Write Better Sentences and Paragraphs

Level 4
English

Previously published as 40 Elaboration Activities That Take Writing from Bland to Brilliant!
Grades 2–4 by Scholastic Inc.

This edition published by Scholastic Education International (Singapore) Private Limited
A division of Scholastic Inc.

First edition 2013

ISBN 978-981-07-5262-0

Welcome to studySM⁺RT !

SCHOLASTIC

Write Better Sentences and Paragraphs provides opportunities for the systematic consolidation and further development of your child's writing skills from word to sentence to paragraph.

It can be a challenge to help children extend their writing skills. The fun and functional topics and variety of engaging exercises in this book will both stimulate and encourage your child to develop the necessary skills to advance as an independent writer. As your child encounters a variety of language and text features, they will learn to select and use the appropriate vocabulary, language structures and techniques for their writing. Your child will also learn to plan, write, proofread and further improve their writing.

Every section targets a specific skill and there is a section at the end of the book with test preparation tips, self-prompting hints, and a self-evaluation checklist.

How to use this book?

1. Introduce the target writing skill at the top of the page to your child.

2. Let your child complete the exercises.

3. Reinforce and extend your child's learning with the tips and activities in the To Parents note, where there is one, at the bottom of the page.

4. Refer to the Test Preparation Tips, Self-Prompting Hints and Self-Evaluation Checklist to consolidate learning.

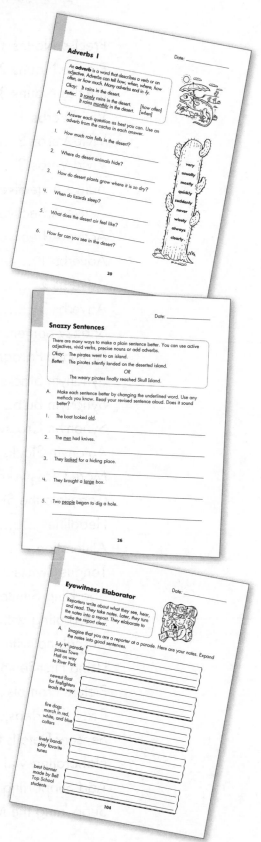

Contents

Precise Nouns 1 6–7

Precise Nouns 2 8

Precise Nouns 3 9

Vivid Verbs 1 10

Vivid Verbs 2 11

Vivid Verbs 3 12–13

Active Adjectives 1 14–15

Active Adjectives 2 16–17

Active Adjectives 3 18–19

Adverbs 1 20

Adverbs 2 21–23

Adverbs 3 24–25

Snazzy Sentences 26–27

Dramatic Paragraphs 28–29

Synonym Stacks 30–31

Synonym Bulb 32

Synonym Crosswords 33–34

Antonym Stacks 35–37

More Crosswords 38–39

Complete the Story 40–41

Headlines 42–43

Alliteration 44–45

Tongue Twisters 46–47

Sparkling Similes 48–49

Elaborating with Metaphors 50–51

Describing with Similes and Metaphors 52–53

Using First-Person and Third-Person Narratives 54–55

Picture Prompts 56–58

Draw for Ideas 59–60

Sensory Details Chart 61–62

Elaborating with the Five Senses 63–64

Add Supporting Details 65–66

Supporting the Main Idea 67–68

Details Diagram 69–70

Dreamy Details 71–72

A Story with Details 73–74

Pet Points 75–76

Detailed Descriptions 77–78

Weather Words 79–80

Add Character Traits 81–82

Dialogue Details 83–85

Build a Sentence 86–87

Support a Main Idea 88–89

Transition Train 90–91

Sentence Stretchers 92–93

Smooth Your Story 94–95

Exaggerate to Elaborate 96–97

The Starting Line 98–99

Linking Paragraphs 100–101

Varying Sentences.. 102–103

Eyewitness Elaborator.................................... 104–105

Writing a News Report.................................... 106–107

Add to an Ad 108–109

Don't Whine...Do Shine! 110–111

Cooking Up a Recipe 112–113

Cooking up a Different Kind of Dish 114–115

Getting Somewhere!....................................... 116–117

Elaboration Editor 118–119

Appealing Anecdote 120–121

Elaborating 122–123

Test Prep Tips 124

Self-Prompting Hints...................................... 125

Elaboration Self-Evaluation Checklist.................... 126

Answers... 127–128

Precise Nouns 1

Nouns are naming words. **Precise** or **exact nouns** name more exactly.
Use better naming words to make your writing more clear.

Okay: My <u>pet</u> likes carrots.

Better: My <u>gerbil</u> likes carrots.

A.   Complete the table below with some examples of more precise nouns. Use the words in the box to help you.

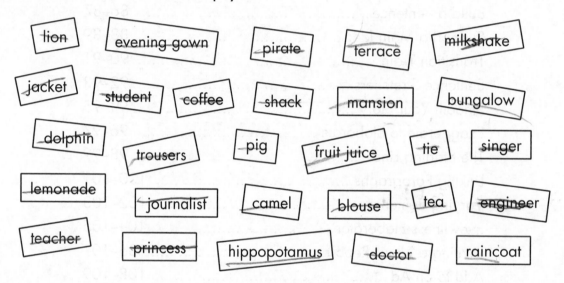

Nouns	Precise Nouns
animal	dolphin, lion, Pig, camel, hippo,
clothing	Jacket, evening gown, trousers, tie, rain coat
drink	lemonade, coffee, fruit juices, tea milk shake (blouse)
house	shack, terrace, mansion, bungalow
person	teacher student, journalists, princess pirate singer Doctor engineer

Can you think of more examples of precise nouns? Add other examples of precise nouns in the table above.

B. Make each sentence better. Look in the box for a better noun. Rewrite the sentence using that more precise noun.

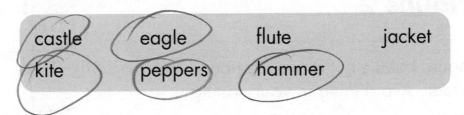

castle   eagle   flute   jacket
kite   peppers   hammer

1. I ate spicy <u>food</u>.

   I ate spicy peppers

2. The <u>bird</u> flew so high.

   The eagle flew so high

3. That old <u>toy</u> lost its tail.

   that old Kite lost its tail

4. You need a <u>tool</u> to fix it.

   You need a hammer to fix it

5. She likes the book's red <u>cover</u>.

   She likes the book's red jacket

6. Let's make a play <u>place</u>.

   let's make a playcastle

7. Jen used to play the <u>instrument</u> in the orchestra.

   Jen used to play the flute in the orchestra

Precise Nouns 2

Thing is a noun, but it's <u>not</u> a precise noun.
Thing is unclear. Avoid *thing* in your writing.

Unclear: Did you join that <u>thing</u>?

Precise: Did you join that <u>club</u>?

Write two different precise nouns to replace each *thing*. Be sure that either noun will make each question clear.

	luggage
box	lougage
back pack	pencil
book	flyer
techneque technique	art style
Dog	basket ball
boom box	Scream
remote	I pad
9x box	play station
car	mini van
toy	hat

1. Will you carry this *THING* for us?

2. Did you leave your *THING* at home?

3. Where is my *THING* on building kites?

4. Have you learned that new *THING* yet?

5. After lunch, will you get the *THING*?

6. How loud can that *THING* go?

7. Which one of you hid that *THING*?

8. Is her *THING* ready yet for the play?

9. Can that *THING* hold all of them?

10. When will his *THING* get here?

Precise Nouns 3

Precise nouns can give more exact names for people, places, and things.

Okay: My uncle lives in a <u>house</u>.

Better: My uncle lives in a <u>cottage</u>.

A.   Give a more precise noun for each plain noun.

Plain noun	Precise noun
1. animal	
2. tree	
3. sport	
4. food	
5. worker	
6. number	
7. room	
8. color	
9. car	
10. machine	

B.   Now pick two of your precise nouns. Use each one in a sentence.

1. _____

2. _____

Vivid Verbs 1

Verbs express action. **Vivid verbs** express action so you can really picture it.

Good: The duck <u>moves</u> to the water.

Better: The duck <u>waddles</u> to the water.

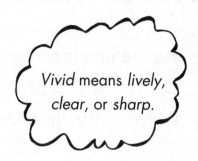

Vivid means lively, clear, or sharp.

Under each picture is a short sentence with a plain verb. Replace each plain verb with a vivid verb. Express the action more sharply.

A horse runs.

1. _____

A cat moves.

2. _____

A child plays.

3. _____

A bell sounds.

4. _____

A dog eats.

5. _____

A girl sees.

6. _____

Music plays.

7. _____

A child draws.

8. _____

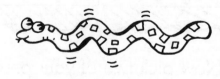

A snake goes.

9. _____

Vivid Verbs 2

> **Vivid verbs** make sentences come to life. They add excitement.
>
> *Okay:*   The arrow <u>hits</u> the target.
>
> *Better:*   The arrow <u>pierces</u> the target.

A.   Each sentence uses a plain verb. Write two or more vivid verbs in the arrow to make the sentence more lively. The first one has been done for you.

1.   Robin Hood takes his best arrow.   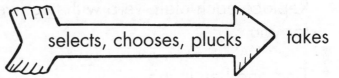 selects, chooses, plucks   takes

2.   He looks at the target.   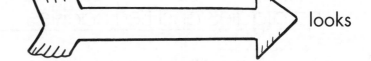   looks

3.   Slowly he closes one eye.   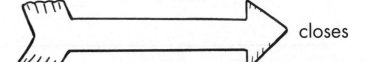   closes

4.   The arrow moves through the air.   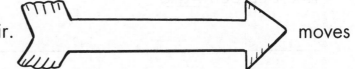   moves

5.   "Yes!" says Robin Hood, with joy.   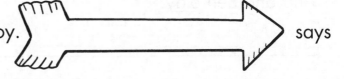   says

6.   He goes to meet his Merry Men.   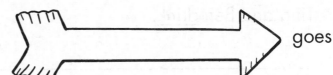   goes

B.   Now write a new sentence about Robin Hood. Use a vivid verb.

_____

Vivid Verbs 3

Vivid verbs are used to fit different people.

Dull: Tina <u>eats</u> and Ben <u>eats</u>.

Better: Tina <u>nibbles</u> and Ben <u>chomps</u>.

A.   Tina and Ben are best friends. Tina is small and neat. Ben is big and active. Read each dull sentence about Tina and Ben. Rewrite the sentence. Replace each plain verb with <u>two</u> lively verbs. The first one has been done for you.

1.   Tina and Ben <u>laugh</u>.

   Tina giggles and Ben cackles.

2.   Tina and Ben <u>talk</u>.

   _____

3.   Tina and Ben <u>walk</u>.

   _____

4.   Tina and Ben <u>play</u>.

   _____

5.   Tina and Ben <u>drink</u>.

   _____

6.   Tina and Ben <u>sing</u>.

   _____

Use vivid verbs to make actions and settings more detailed and interesting. Choose verbs that paint vivid pictures.

B.   Use vivid verbs to rewrite each of the descriptions and make them more interesting and alive. Try not to use the same vivid verb again.

Paragraph 1:

One morning, as Jeannie was <u>going</u> out of her house, she <u>saw</u> Fiona <u>going</u> down the lane. Fiona was <u>singing</u> to herself quietly as she <u>went</u> along. In her left hand, she <u>had</u> a bouquet of flowers. "Where's Fiona going to?" <u>thought</u> Jeannie.

_____

_____

_____

_____

Paragraph 2:

I <u>like</u> parks. You can <u>sit</u> on one of the benches with a book and <u>see</u> the world go by. Families would be <u>having</u> picnics on the grass and dogs would be <u>running</u> in the sun while their owners <u>sit</u> around. When the ice-cream man <u>comes</u>, the children would <u>go</u> to get a cone, then go <u>playing</u> in the lake and <u>shouting</u> in delight.

_____

_____

_____

_____

To parents   On a separate sheet of paper, pick out five verbs your child has written above. Ask him or her to write down an alternative vivid verb to each of the five verbs and make a sentence with each of them.

13

Active Adjectives 1

Adjectives are words that describe nouns. Strong adjectives spark the imagination. They give readers clear pictures in their minds as they read. Use active adjectives to make your writing more interesting.

Okay: She sat under a tree.

Better: She sat under a <u>leafy</u> tree.

A.   Look at the following picture. Can you think of words to describe the different things in the picture? Complete the graphic organizer below.

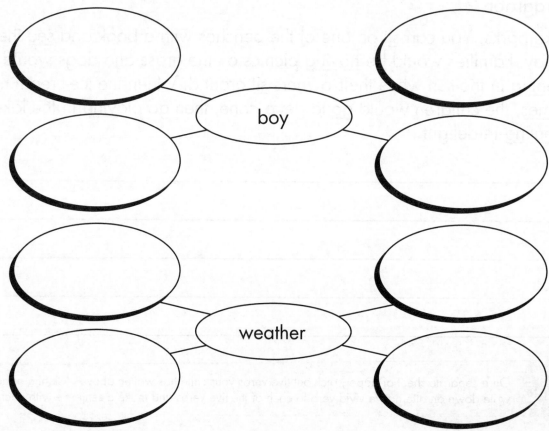

boy

weather

14

B. Think about each word in the web. In the spaces around it, write adjectives to describe the word.

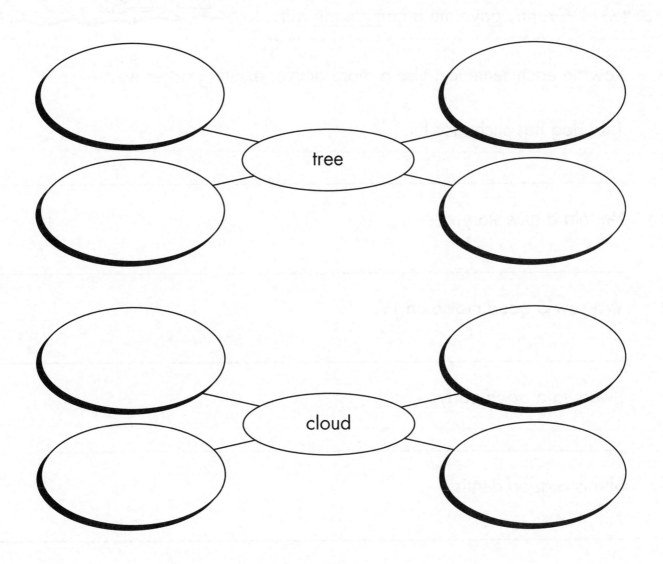

tree

cloud

Active Adjectives 2

Nice is an adjective. *Good* is an adjective, too. But both are boring. Why? The adjectives *nice* and *good* aren't clear. People use *nice* and *good* too often. You can do better!

Boring: Granny gave me a <u>nice</u> gift.

Better: Granny gave me a <u>homemade</u> gift.

A.   Rewrite each sentence. Use a more active, exciting adjective.

1.   That dog has such *nice* fur.

_____

2.   He told a *nice* story.

_____

3.   We saw a *good* movie on TV.

_____

4.   I went to a *good* party.

_____

5.   She is a *good* dentist.

_____

To parents   Ask your child to write a story or paragraph using an exaggeration as the beginning of the story. Suggest to your child to think big and over the top!

B. Rewrite the following paragraph. Use more active, exciting adjectives to replace the underlined words. You can use more than one adjective to replace the underlined words.

I went to Japan for my holiday and it was such a <u>good</u> holiday. We saw a lot of <u>nice</u> cherry blossoms and <u>nice</u> temples. The scenery was simply nice. The seafood that we had on the trip was really <u>good</u>. I wish we had such <u>nice</u> seafood back home. We also saw a lot of <u>nice</u> souvenirs and tidbits. All the tidbits we saw had <u>nice</u>, individual packaging. I wish I could buy a little bit of everything home. It was a <u>good</u> trip and I wish I could go back there again.

_____

_____

_____

_____

_____

_____

_____

_____

Active Adjectives 3

> **Adjectives** can describe the same idea in different ways. Think about adjectives that describe size:
>
> *Small:*   He took a <u>tiny</u> bite of the pie.
>
> *Medium:* He took a <u>healthy</u> bite of the pie.
>
> *Large:*   He took an <u>enormous</u> bite of the pie.

A.   Fill in the adjective steps. As the steps rise, use more dramatic adjectives.

1.   Adjectives about <u>happiness</u>:

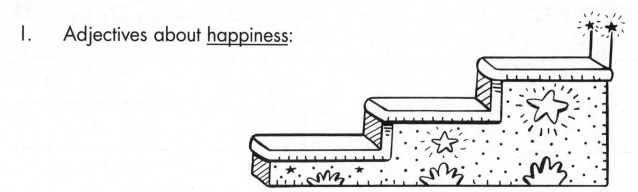

2.   Adjectives about <u>height</u>:

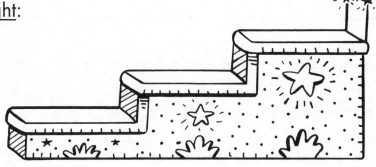

3.   Adjectives about <u>sound</u>:

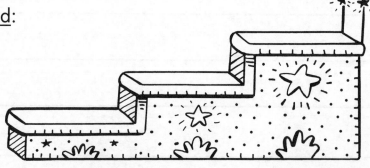

B. Complete the following descriptions with the most suitable adjectives.
Use the words in the box to help you.

| hungry | famished | peckish | parched | dry |
| arid | terrified | scared | startled | |

Perry was _____! He had not eaten anything for days. His throat

was _____ as his water had run out. He wanted to call for help

but his phone had run out of battery. Alone and _____, Perry

wanted to cry but he had no more tears left. He could only hope that someone

would notice that he was missing and come to look for him.

Crystal was _____. She had already eaten her dinner but she still

felt unsatisfied. Maybe she should have a nice, warm cup of hot chocolate.

After all, her throat felt a little _____ and the warm drink would

fill her up. As she reached for the jar of chocolate, a gecko sprang out from

behind the jar and _____ her. It gave her such a shock!

As the travelers journeyed in the hot and _____ desert, they

started to get _____. They hoped to reach the oasis soon so that

they could eat and rest. They knew that they needed to break soon and were

_____ of running out of strength so early in the journey.

Adverbs 1

An **adverb** is a word that describes a verb or an adjective. Adverbs can tell *how, when, where, how often,* or *how much.* Many adverbs end in *-ly.*

Okay: It rains in the desert.

Better: It <u>rarely</u> rains in the desert.   [*how often*]
It rains <u>monthly</u> in the desert.   [*when*]

A.   Answer each question as best you can. Use an adverb from the cactus in each answer.

1.   How much rain falls in the desert?

_____

2.   Where do desert animals hide?

_____

3.   How do desert plants grow where it is so dry?

_____

4.   When do lizards sleep?

_____

5.   What does the desert air feel like?

_____

6.   How far can you see in the desert?

_____

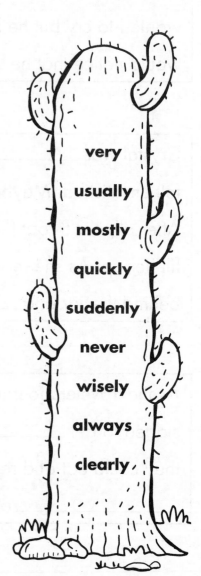

very

usually

mostly

quickly

suddenly

never

wisely

always

clearly

Adverbs 2

Adverbs give more details to verbs by telling *how*, *when*, *where*, *how often*, or *how much*. Adverbs go <u>before</u> or <u>after</u> the word they describe.

Okay: Matt read my story.

Better: Matt <u>carefully</u> read my story.   [*before*]

   Matt read my story <u>slowly</u>.   [*after*]

A.   Fill in the blanks with adverbs from the box below.

boastfully   bravely   diligently   doubtfully

dreamily   hungrily   longingly   triumphantly

1.   Being a conscientious boy, Jason always does his work _____.

2.   The rich lady said _____, "I'm throwing the grandest party in town!"

3.   Natalie was gazing _____ across the field instead of paying attention in class.

4.   The football team whooped _____ when they won the game.

5.   Although it was a tough hike up the mountain, the boys took up the challenge _____.

6.   "Seriously, I don't think that is a good idea," Ivan shook his head _____.

21

7.   Feeling ravenous, Jimmy gobbled down his dinner _____.

8.   Melanie looked _____ at the delicious desserts in the

     ice-cream shop.

B.   Read each sentence about Lee. Write an
     adverb in the space to make the sentence
     better. The first one has been done for you.

 1. Lee _____messily_____ cooks dinner
     for me.

 2. Lee sleeps _____ in his
     bunk bed.

 3. Lee _____ dances to
     the music.

 4. Lee _____ peeked out the window.

 5. Lee paints the fence _____.

 6. Lee _____ throws a stick for his dog.

 7. Lee says his lines _____ in the play.

 8. Lee _____ calls his grandfather on Sundays.

 9. At the party, Lee _____ opened his gifts.

10. Lee said goodbye _____ to his friend.

C. Read the stories below. Underline the adverbs in the stories.

Christmas Shopping

The Christmas decorations were glittering beautifully in the shopping mall while snow drifted outside the windows. Susan was busily shopping for presents.

She carefully picked up a glass vase and examined it closely. "It's perfect for Mum!" she thought delightedly.

Always Late!

Lindsey was waiting impatiently at the bus stop. "The bus is always late!" she grumbled moodily.

Tony came along. He cheerfully greeted Lindsey, "Good morning, Lindsey! Why do you look so glum?"

"I am going to be late for violin lessons," Lindsey sighed resignedly.

"Well, it happens sometimes," Tony suggested helpfully. "Cheer up, it will arrive soon."

To parents On a separate sheet of paper, get your child to write three more sentences to continue one of the above stories. Ask him or her to use adverbs to make them more interesting.

Adverbs 3

Adverbs can help you to describe *how* a person speaks. We make most adverbs by adding *–ly* to an adjective. If the adjective ends with 'y', we have to drop the 'y' and add 'ily'.

Okay: "I'm ready," said Tracy.

Better: "I'm ready," said Tracy <u>nervously</u>.

A. Complete the table and form the adverb that can describe *how* a person speaks.

Adjective	Adverb	Adjective	Adverb
angry		loud	
calm		polite	
cautious		quiet	
eager		rude	
exasperated		soft	
glad		sudden	
happy		thoughtful	
hasty		warm	

B. Add an adverb to better describe how each person is speaking.

1. We blindfolded Jane and led her down the staircase. Everyone was waiting to surprise her. "Are we there yet?" asked Jane _____.

2. "The clowns are here!" said Hakim _____ as he jumped up and down in delight.

3. "Are you nuts?" said Asher _____, "I don't think we should be doing this."

4. "Why did you bring them along?" asked Bradley _____. He had told her many times to leave her pets at home but again, she had not listened.

5. "You forgot your lunch again," said Kyle _____. He was tired of reminding Mina about everything!

6. "I baked another pie," said Eva _____. She was really satisfied with the pies she had baked and how much her family and friends enjoyed them.

7. "When can we go swimming?" asked Jared _____. He had been looking forward to going swimming for a long time and Dad had promised to bring him.

8. She was already late and Sally was still taking her own sweet time. "Get in the car right now!" said Mom _____.

9. "I lost my homework," said Hannah _____. She had spent all night working on it and left it in the bus.

10. "May I hold the lizard?" asked Zane _____. He wanted to experience something new even though it made him feel a little frightened.

Snazzy Sentences

There are many ways to make a plain sentence better. You can use active adjectives, vivid verbs, precise nouns or add adverbs.

Okay: The pirates went to an island.

Better: The pirates silently landed on the deserted island.

OR

The weary pirates finally reached Skull Island.

A.   Make each sentence better by changing the underlined word. Use any methods you know. Read your revised sentence aloud. Does it sound better?

1.   The boat looked <u>old</u>.

_____

2.   The <u>men</u> had knives.

_____

3.   They <u>looked</u> for a hiding place.

_____

4.   They brought a <u>large</u> box.

_____

5.   Two <u>people</u> began to dig a hole.

_____

6. Another <u>person</u> started to <u>draw</u> a map.

_____

7. "Leave no clues!" <u>said</u> the leader.

_____

B. Now, look at the sentences in Part A again. Can you add more details or adverbs to make them even more exciting? Improve the sentences and rewrite them as a paragraph below.

_____

_____

_____

_____

_____

_____

_____

_____

_____

Dramatic Paragraphs

A good paragraph keeps your readers hooked to read more. This can be achieved by adding suitable describing words and adverbs to make your content more interesting and vivid.

A.   Rewrite and improve each paragraph by replacing the underlined words with vivid verbs. Try not to repeat your verbs.

1.   One morning, Mary was <u>going</u> past a grocery store. She had <u>had</u> her swimming lesson. Suddenly, she heard a child <u>crying</u>. She turned and saw a little girl <u>crying</u>.

_____

_____

_____

_____

2.   "What's wrong?" Mary <u>said</u>. "I've lost my money for lunch!" the child <u>said</u>. "Don't cry. Here's some money so you can get something to eat," Mary <u>gave</u> some money to the little girl. The little girl stopped crying and <u>smiled</u> at Mary. Mary felt glad as she watched the little girl <u>go</u> away.

_____

_____

_____

_____

B. Rewrite each paragraph in Part A by adding adverbs to the verbs you changed. You can place the adverbs <u>before</u> or <u>after</u> the verbs. Try not to repeat your adverbs.

_____

_____

_____

_____

_____

_____

_____

_____

_____

_____

_____

_____

To parents On a separate sheet of paper, get your child to write a short paragraph about a good deed he or she has done or would like to do using vivid verbs and interesting adverbs to make their writing dramatic and interesting.

Synonym Stacks

Synonyms are words that mean the same, or nearly the same. You can make your writing better by using synonyms.

Okay: That mask may <u>scare</u> little kids.

Better: That mask may <u>terrify</u> little kids.

A. Read all the words in the box. Write the synonyms where they belong.

anyone	being	bitter	bleak	character	cheery
chilly	creature	contented	frosty	frozen	glad
human	jolly	joyful	member	pleased	arctic
thrilled	wintry	somebody	blissful	nippy	

Synonyms for HAPPY	Synonyms for PERSON	Synonyms for COLD

30

B.   There are also many synonyms for verbs. Look at the synonyms in the box.
     Write the synonyms where they belong.

stroll	jog	sprint	snivel
tread	gobble	dash	chuckle
hop	howl	saunter	yell
leap	cackle	giggle	stride
spring	shout	swallow	scurry
skip	screech	munch	bounce
wander	shriek	guffaw	

Synonyms for RUN	Synonyms for WALK	Synonyms for SCREAM

Synonyms for LAUGH	Synonyms for EAT	Synonyms for JUMP

Synonym Bulb

Some words have many **synonyms**.

Plain word: mistake

Synonyms: error, blunder, slip-up, confusion

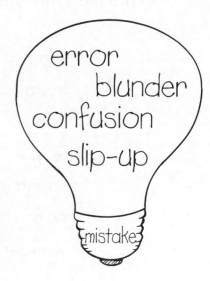

Use this light-bulb chart to list synonyms. Write a starting word in the base of the bulb. List synonyms in the round part of the bulb. Work on your own or with a partner.

word

Synonym Crosswords

Synonyms are words that have the same or nearly the same meaning.

A. Complete the crossword puzzle below with synonyms of the clue words. Use the letters provided in the puzzle to help you.

Across

2. pleasant
4. mistake
6. crazy
7. great
9. pretty

Down

1. bluff
3. funny
5. decay
8. happy
10. real

B. Complete the crossword puzzle below with words to complete each sentence.

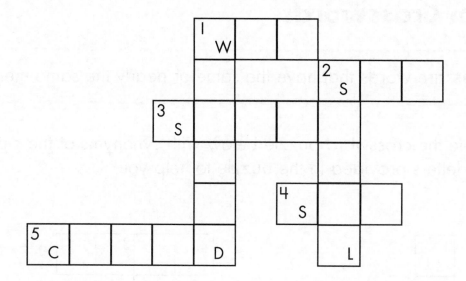

Across

1. The tennis star _____ the match beating his opponent.

2. Grandpa _____ in his chair and read his newspapers.

3. The tired girl _____ soundly through the night.

4. Kenny was _____ because he lost his ball in the park.

5. The baby _____ as he was hungry.

Down

1. She _____ down the stairs and ran all the way to the bus stop.

2. The robber was caught trying to _____ from the old man.

Antonym Stacks

> **Antonyms** are words that have the opposite meaning.
>
> *Word:*   happy
>
> *Antonyms:*   sad, unhappy, gloomy, miserable

A.   Read all the words in the box. Write the antonyms where they belong.

failure	unfriendly	warm	sincere	catastrophe
unkind	disappointment	flop	hostile	sizzling
nasty	unfeeling	kind	friendly	harsh
spiteful	loving	tender	let down	thermal

Antonyms for PLEASANT	Antonyms for SUCCESS	Antonyms for COLD

B.   Look at the paragraphs below. What antonyms can you think of that show opposite meanings to the underlined words?

Craig was a <u>tall</u> and <u>strong</u> boy. In fact, he was tallest in his class. He was also <u>athletic</u> and was on the track and field team. He was <u>liked</u> by many because he was <u>friendly</u>, <u>helpful</u> and <u>cheerful</u>. One of the most <u>popular</u> boys in school, his teachers found him to be <u>humble</u> and <u>hardworking</u>. His parents always said that he made them very <u>proud</u>. Make a list of antonyms for the underlined words.

Now, make a list of antonyms for the underlined words.

WORD	ANTONYM
tall	
strong	
athletic	
liked	
friendly	
helpful	
cheerful	
popular	
humble	
hardworking	
proud	

C. Rewrite the paragraph in Part B using some of the antonyms listed in Part A to replace the underlined words. Then replace the name of the character to create a new character.

_____

_____

_____

_____

_____

_____

_____

_____

_____

_____

_____

_____

_____

_____

More Crosswords

A. Complete the crossword puzzle below using the clues provided.

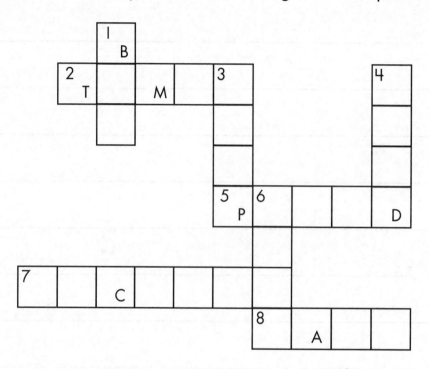

Across

2. The brothers were so different – one was so brave, the other was so
    _____.

5. This word has a similar meaning to snobbish.

7. An antonym of fail.

8. A synonym of simple.

Down

1. An antonym for small.

3. This side of the pool is too _____ for you. You should go to
    the shallow side.

4. The children were so _____ and noisy.

6. The opposite of polite.

B.   Now create your own crossword in the box below and add your own clues.

Across

Down

Complete the Story

A. This story has many missing words. Read it. Think about how to make it better. Fill in each blank. Use words from the box below. (Note: Words can be used more than once.)

siblings	buddies	build	crowded	eagerly
space	furniture	entrance	hideaway	sisters
homey	hosted	lumber	cushions	

A Place of Our Own

Pablo and Theo are neighbors. They have been (1) _____ since they were four years old. Pablo has five (2) _____. He is the only son. Theo lives with seven (3) _____. "It's way too (4) _____ at our houses. We need some kind of (5) _____ just for us," the boys said. So they made plans. They decided to build a private (6) _____. There was room for one in Theo's yard.

First the boys got scraps of (7) _____ and pieces of (8) _____. Pablo's mom showed them how to (9) _____ sturdy walls. Theo's uncle helped them make a good (10) _____ with a window in it.

"Now we need some (11) _____ for the inside," the boys agreed. So they looked (12) _____ through the attic. They hoped to find items to make their place feel more (13) _____. Pablo found some old, soft (14) _____ that his mother no longer wanted. When they were done, Pablo and Theo (15) _____ a small party.

B.   Now, think of some words of your own to replace the words in the blanks. Then rewrite the story. You can choose your own characters and change some of the details in the story to create your own story. Look at the example provided below.

Our Playhouse

Gina and I are neighbors. We have been <u>best friends</u> since we were in diapers. Both of us have four <u>siblings</u>. "It's way too <u>noisy</u> at our houses. We need some kind of <u>playhouse</u> just for us," we agreed....

_____

_____

_____

_____

_____

_____

_____

_____

_____

_____

To parents Provide your child with other missing-word stories and get your child to complete the stories. You may want to provide a word basket to help your child.

41

Headlines

A **headline** is the title of a newspaper story. It gives the main idea in a few words. A good headline grabs your attention. It makes you want to read more.

Dull: Early Morning Snow Falls

Better: Roosters Shiver in Dawn Blizzard

A.   Look at the following headlines. What do you think each story is about? Write your answer in the blanks. Which ones catch your attention and make you want to read more?

| Britain Hit by Storm of the Century | _____ |

| Driver Crashes Into Tree | _____ |

| Just Point – The Latest in Camera Technology | _____ |

| Golfer Wins Championship | _____ |

B.   Write better headlines. Make each one SHORT and SHARP. Use six words or less. Be creative! The first one has been done for you.

1.   President Gives Speech   { President's Speech Excites Young Voters }

2.   New Theme Park Opens   { }

3. Exciting Sports News

4. Great New Invention

5. Adventure Movie Opens

6. Child Wins Big Prize

7. Rush Hour Traffic Jam

8. Astronaut Visits Town

Alliteration

Alliteration is repeating the beginning sound in a string of words. You can use alliteration to make your writing sound more interesting.

No alliteration: Marla builds movie disguises.

Alliteration: <u>M</u>arla <u>m</u>akes <u>m</u>onster <u>m</u>ovie <u>m</u>asks.

A.   You can choose adjectives that have the same starting letter as a character's name. The adjective you choose can give an idea of the character's personality. Look at the pictures and think of possible words that start with the same sound to describe each character. The first one has been done for you.

1.

Messy Maggie

2.

_____ Ned

3.

_____ Terry

4.

_____ Grandpa

5.

_____ Priscilla

6.

_____ Fred

B. Use each word given in a 3- to 5-word phrase.
    Make all the words start with the same sound.
    The first one has been done as an example.

1. baby
    bathing baby blowing bubbles
    _____

2. chewy

    _____

3. dress

    _____

4. fish

    _____

5. jelly

    _____

6. machine

    _____

To parents Challenge your child to write fully alliterative sentences for Part B.

45

Tongue Twisters

Alliteration is used in **tongue twisters**. Tongue twisters help improve our pronunciation in a fun way.

Okay: <u>S</u>ix <u>s</u>wans <u>s</u>wam.

Better: <u>S</u>ix <u>s</u>illy <u>s</u>wans <u>s</u>wam <u>s</u>wiftly.

A.   Make up some tongue twisters. Use each letter given. Follow this plan.

What Kind?	Who or What?	Did What?	How?
Six silly	swans	swam	swiftly

1.   N

_____

2.   F

_____

3.   T

_____

4.   L

_____

5.   R

_____

6.   Q

_____

B. Let's create two-line tongue twisters using the words given below. Think up more alliteration to complete your tongue twisters.

1.

| say | sheep | sidewalk | sitting |

_____

_____

_____

2.

| three | ticked | timer | train |

_____

_____

_____

3.

| Dan | deep | ditch | duck |

_____

_____

_____

Sparking Similes

A **simile** compares two things. Some similes compare two things using the word *like* or the structure *as* _____ *as*.

Okay: The athlete runs fast.

Better: The athlete runs <u>like a jackrabbit</u>.

OR The athlete runs <u>as fast as the wind</u>.

A. What can you compare the following objects / items to? What qualities do you associate with the objects / items? Brainstorm and complete the table below. The first one has been done for you.

	Main thing	Can be compared to...
1.	Ballerina dancing	A graceful swan
2.	Girl pecking at her food	
3.	Children fighting	
4.	A busy worker	
5.	A person with fair skin	
6.	A wise person	

B. Use what you have written in the table above to complete the similes below.

1. The ballerina was as _____ as a swan.

2. The girl eats like a _____.

3. They were fighting like _____.

4. The worker was as busy as _____.

5. She was so fair, her skin was as _____.

6. He was wise like _____.

C. Make each sentence better. Compare two things with a simile that uses 'like'.

1. She reads eagerly.

_____

2. The wizard flies around.

_____

3. Uncle Arnold walks slowly.

_____

4. The water sparkles in the sun.

_____

5. His bookshelf is starting to sag.

_____

6. The deer darts through the woods.

_____

Elaborating with Metaphors

Metaphors compare one idea to another by drawing on their similarities.

Okay: Her eyes are sparkling.

Better: Her eyes are jewels in the sun.

Here 'sparkling' is replaced by a visual of jewels sparkling in the sun, which gives readers a clearer image in their minds.

A.   Make each sentence better. Rewrite each sentence by replacing the underlined phrases with suitable metaphors from the box.

cats and dogs	frozen with fear	daggers through my heart
shining star	sent my heart racing	

1.   He was <u>scared stiff</u> in the haunted house.

_____

2.   It has been raining <u>heavily</u> since yesterday!

_____

3.   Those mean words that Joe said were <u>hurting me deeply</u>.

_____

4.   Bob is the <u>most outstanding person</u> of our school.

_____

5.   The wonderful news <u>made me feel excited</u>.

_____

B. Rewrite each sentence by replacing the underlined phrases with suitable metaphors of your own.

1. Larry was bored so he felt time was <u>passing very slowly</u>.

   _____

2. She tried to run away but her legs were <u>wobbly</u>.

   _____

3. Tina was so nervous that she <u>could not say anything.</u>

   _____

4. There was no teacher in the classroom so the students were <u>mischievously playing</u> around.

   _____

   _____

5. The <u>wrinkled and shrunken</u> old man hobbled slowly across the road.

   _____

   _____

6. Kathy's voice was so beautiful it was <u>sweet sounding</u>.

   _____

   _____

Describing with Similes and Metaphors

Similes and metaphors can be used to make your descriptions of people and places more vivid in your reader's minds.

A.   Tick one of the categories below. Decide on a person in that category you wish to write about.

I want to write about:

❏ A Local Sports Hero   ❏ A Popular Movie Celebrity   ❏ An American President
❏ A Scientist or Inventor   ❏ A Famous Historian

The person I want to write about is: _____

Think of the person's characteristics and write suitable similes and metaphors to describe them in the table provided.

Characteristic	Similes and Metaphors

Use the similes and metaphors above to write a paragraph about this person.

_____

_____

_____

_____

_____

B. Tick one of the categories below, then decide on a place in that category you wish to write about. You may wish to use a photograph to help you write suitable similes and metaphors to describe it.

I want to write about:

- ❏ A place in my neighborhood
- ❏ A place of interest I have visited
- ❏ A place of interest I want to visit
- ❏ A favorite hangout
- ❏ Others: _____

Name of this place: _____

Think of the characteristics of this place and write suitable similes and metaphors to describe them in the table provided.

Characteristic	Similes and Metaphors

Use the similes and metaphors above to write a paragraph about this place.

_____

_____

_____

_____

_____

To parents Pick another category from the above selection and get your child to think of a place in this category. On a separate sheet of paper, create a publicity poster for this place using similes and metaphors.

Using First-Person and Third-Person Narratives

A **first-person narrative** is written from the viewpoint of a participant in an event. A **third-person narrative** is written from the viewpoint of an on-looker.

A. Rewrite the sentences below in the first-person by replacing the underlined words with the words in brackets.

1. She always prepares <u>his</u> favorite food for <u>their</u> dinner. (my, our)

_____

_____

2. <u>Jancy and Jane</u> enjoy chatting with <u>their</u> grandparents. (We, our)

_____

_____

B. Rewrite the sentences below in the third-person by replacing the underlined words with the words in brackets.

1. It was the first day of school and <u>I</u> absolutely enjoyed it. (Sally)

_____

_____

2. <u>I</u> think nothing is impossible if <u>I</u> persevere in it. (Vincent, he)

_____

_____

C. Read the following texts. Decide if they are written in first-person or third-person narrative. Then rewrite the text in the other narrative voice using the words in brackets.

1.

> When we landed, I saw very green trees bearing colorful fruit and flowers. I saw the sun shining brightly in a cloudless sky. I was so excited to have made this trip with Henry and Cassie that I felt a sudden urge to let out a whoop of joy. (Jessie, he, they)

Narrative type: _____

_____

_____

_____

_____

2.

> John heard some noise in the streets below and looked out of his window curiously. He saw some people getting out of a lorry and realized that they were his new neighbors. He recognized one of them as his classmate and best friend, Clarissa. He was delighted because they would be able to go to school together. (I, my, we)

Narrative type: _____

_____

_____

_____

_____

To parents Get your child to pick out a paragraph from a favorite book. Decide if it is written in the first-person or third-person narrative. On a separate sheet of paper, ask your child to rewrite it in the other narrative voice.

Picture Prompts

Pictures can be used to help create a clearer visual image and mood so that writers have a clearer idea of the setting and feelings of characters.

A. Select one of the pictures below and circle it. Describe the setting and feelings in the space below and create a short paragraph about the picture using your descriptions.

Where is this place? Describe what it looks like. You can use similes and metaphors.

_____

_____

_____

How do the people feel in this picture?

_____

_____

_____

Let's put your descriptions into a paragraph:

_____

_____

_____

_____

B. Paste an interesting photograph that shows an activity with lots of people such as a party or a celebration. Describe the setting and feelings in the space below and create a short paragraph about the photograph using your descriptions.

Paste your interesting photograph here:

Where is this place? Describe what it looks like. You can use similes and metaphors.

_____

_____

_____

How do the people feel in this picture?

_____

_____

_____

Let's put your descriptions into a paragraph:

_____

_____

_____

_____

_____

_____

To parents Go through a favorite photo album. Now ask your child to think of a simile or metaphor to describe each photograph as you view it. Share them with your family.

Draw for Ideas

It's often said, "A picture is worth a thousand words."

One way to get ideas for writing is to draw a picture. Many writing ideas can come from your own artwork.

A.   Pick a topic. Draw picture about it.

Topic: _____

B.   Now think of some words and ideas based on your artwork and list them
      below.

Words and Ideas:

_____

_____

_____

_____

_____

C.   Now use the words and ideas you have listed to write a short paragraph
      about your topic.

_____

_____

_____

_____

_____

_____

_____

Sensory Details Chart

> **Details** are small parts about something larger. Our senses help us take in details about the world. The five senses are *seeing*, *touching*, *hearing*, *tasting*, and *smelling*.

A. Pick an object. Think about how your senses would respond to it. List words to describe the object for each of your five senses. (Warning: Do NOT taste anything without asking first!)

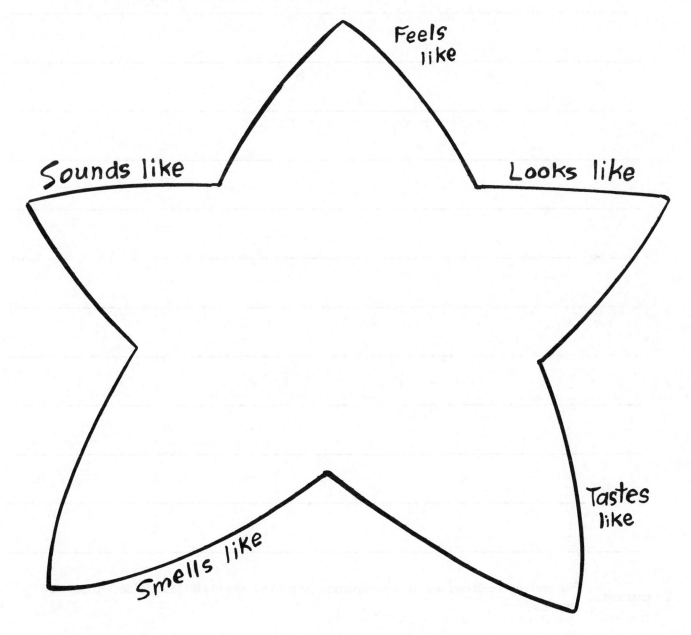

B.   Now, write a short description of the object you chose in the lines below. Use what you have listed in the star on the previous page. Remember that you can also use similes or metaphors in your description.

Sense of Touch: Smooth and cool

Description: The (object) was as smooth as silk and it was cool to the touch.

_____

_____

_____

_____

_____

_____

_____

_____

_____

_____

_____

_____

To parents   Pick another object and use the same approach to get your child to brainstorm ideas to describe the object.

Elaborating with the Five Senses

Using all your five senses to describe a picture or visual image can help you paint a more complete picture when you write.

A.   Write down what you would see, hear, smell, feel and taste in each scenario. Use your imagination and suitable describing words and phrases.

Sunset at the beach	
What can you see?	
What can you hear?	
What can you smell?	
What can you taste?	
What can you feel?	

Indoor Basketball Match	
What can you see?	
What can you hear?	
What can you smell?	
What can you taste?	
What can you feel?	

Hustle Bustle!

B.   Cut out or print a photograph of a busy place and paste it here:

+---+
| |
| |
| |
| Paste your photograph here: |
| |
| |
| |
| |
+---+

Now, imagine that you are at the place in the photograph. Write down what you would see, hear, smell, taste, and feel.

What can you see?	
What can you hear?	
What can you smell?	
What can you taste?	
What can you feel?	

To parents   Using the details written above, get your child to create a short but descriptive paragraph about the place described. Get your family or friends to give more ideas to make it better.

Add Supporting Details

Use details that support an idea to make your writing clearer.

Dull: Fred hated his lunch.

Better: Fred hated his lunch <u>because</u> it was another greasy meatloaf
         sandwich.

A.   Read each part of a sentence. Match each idea with a suitable detail to
      support it.

1.   The school organized a treasure
      hunt

•   all around the school
     compound.

2.   The teachers hid the small tokens

•   for Children's Day.

3.   The children were very excited

•   because they all wanted
     to get the prizes.

4.   Some of the children ran to the
      playground

•   as everyone got a prize.

5.   At the end of the day all the
      children were happy

•   to look for the prizes the
     teachers hid.

B.   Now rewrite the sentences above in a paragraph.

_____

_____

_____

_____

_____

_____

_____

_____

C.   Read each sentence. Look for a clue you can use to add supporting details. Rewrite the sentence using the details. Give a complete idea.

1.   The boys did not want to go to the museum _____

_____.

2.   They made up stories _____

_____.

3.   Nobody noticed the time _____

_____.

4.   The bus stopped in front _____

_____.

5.   The boys rushed off _____

_____.

6.   They never expected to see those _____

_____.

Supporting the Main Idea

Use **graphic organizers** to reorganize supporting information into groups of related points when writing about a main idea. This will give you a neater and clearer explanation of your main idea.

You are writing a report on "Niagara Falls" and have the following a publicity brochure on this tourist attraction.

NIAGARA FALLS

The Niagara Falls is found on the border of Ontario, Canada and New York, USA. It was created by glaciers almost 10,000 years ago and produces the highest flow rate of any waterfall on earth.

It is made up of three waterfalls, the American Falls, the Bridal Veil Falls, and the Horseshoe Falls. The largest is the Horseshoe Falls and the smallest is the Bridal Veil Falls. The largest vertical drop of the Niagara Falls is over 165 feet! Though a number of people have attempted to go over the Niagara Falls, it is illegal to do so.

The Niagara Falls is a popular place of interest. Visitors can view the American Falls from Prospect Point Park. You can also go to Bridal Veil Falls from the Cave of the Winds. Other attractions are the Three Sisters Islands and the Power Portal, where a huge statue of Nikola Tesla can be seen.

The Niagara Scenic Trolley also provides guided trips along the American Falls. Get panoramic views of the falls from the Flight of Angels helium balloon ride, or by helicopter. Did you know that the Niagara Falls State Park is the oldest state park in the United States? Visit the Niagara Falls with your family today!

Now, organize the information in the brochure into the graphic organizer below.

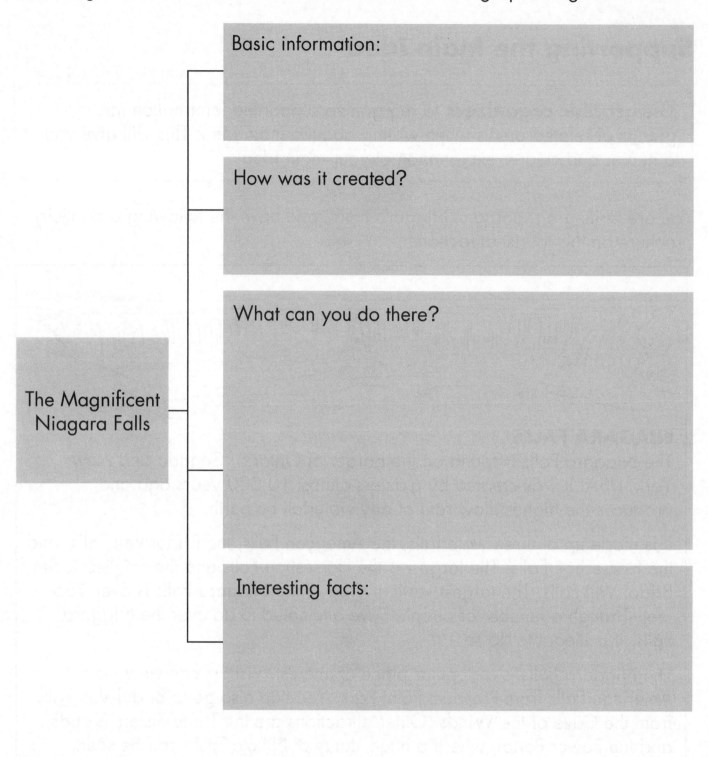

Basic information:

How was it created?

What can you do there?

The Magnificent Niagara Falls

Interesting facts:

To parents Using the information in your graphic organizer, get your child to write a report on "The Magnificent Niagara Falls" using suitable vivid verbs, adverbs, similes and metaphors to make the report more interesting.

Details Diagram

Adding details makes a story better. There are many kinds of details. Use the diagram below to collect ideas.

A.   Think about the categories listed in the table. Use the questions to help you. Then list words or ideas for your story where they belong in the table.

Pick a story topic: _____

Category	Details
Setting: *Where does your story take place?*	• *What does the setting look like?* • *Were there any particular weather conditions?*
People: *Who are the main and secondary characters?*	• *What are the names of the characters?* • *What are the characters like?* • *Will something special happen to the characters?*
Things: *Was there anything important for your topic?*	• *What things play a part in your story?* • *Describe these things.*
Senses: *Which of your five senses would you use for your story?*	• *List the ideas that target the different senses.*

B. Now use some of the details that you have listed to write a paragraph about your topic. It could be a short story or it could be a description of an object, person or an event.

_____

_____

_____

_____

_____

_____

_____

_____

_____

_____

_____

_____

_____

To parents Get your child to think of other topics to brainstorm ideas about. You can use the same categories provided.

Dreamy Details

Everybody dreams. But the details from a dream can be unclear. Use the chart below to collect ideas. Add details that make sense.

Tell the main idea of a dream / story: _____

List words or ideas in the dreamy detail chart. Use the categories listed below to help you. Use one bubble per category.

Categories: Setting / People / Feelings / Events / Things

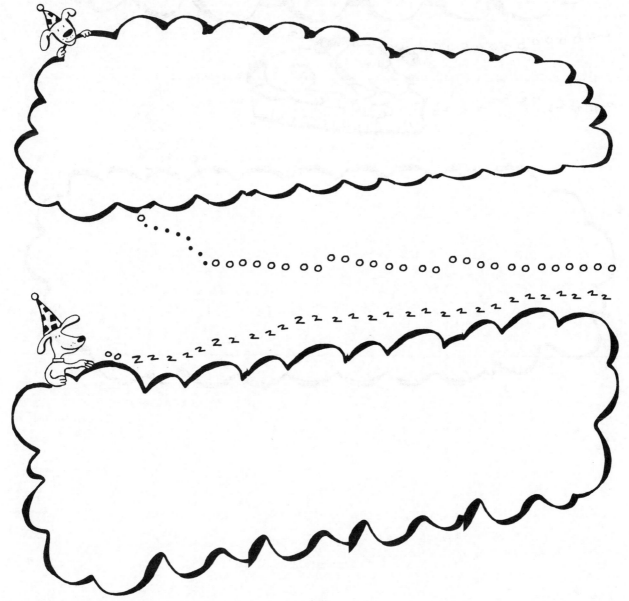

A Story with Details

When writing a narrative, you are telling a story. It can be told from a first-person or third-person perspective. Using a graphic organizer will help you organize the beginning, middle and end of your narrative.

A. Pick an experience you have had and fill in a suitable word for the title. Then follow the steps to write a good narrative.

A/An _____ Incident

Which voice are you writing in? First-Person / Third-Person (Circle accordingly)

Write down information about this incident in the graphic organizer below.

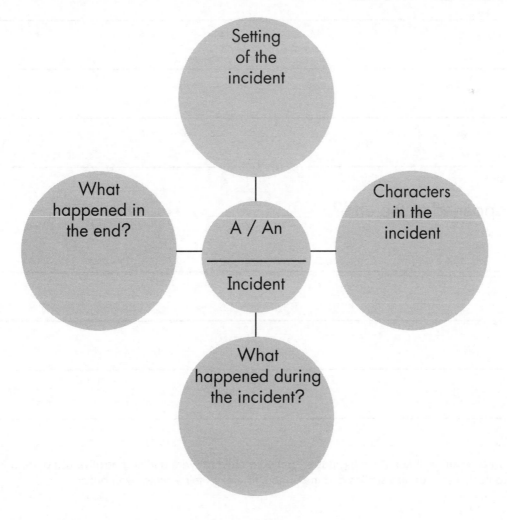

B. Elaborate on your points by using cues from your five senses. Write them in the space below.

Setting and Characters:

_____

_____

_____

_____

What happened during the incident?

_____

_____

_____

_____

_____

What happened in the end?

_____

_____

_____

_____

_____

To parents On a separate sheet of writing paper, get your child to write out the narrative using the above content. They can use similes and metaphors to make their writing even better.

Pet Points

Do you have a pet? Do you want a pet? Either way, you can gather details to write about pets.

A. Categorize the points below into the different categories to describe a pet. Then write down the type of pet in the center.

yelps	pounces	tiny	Snowball	short round tail
soft	meows	milk	fluffy	like a ball of cotton
stealthily	fish	purrs	biscuits	milky white

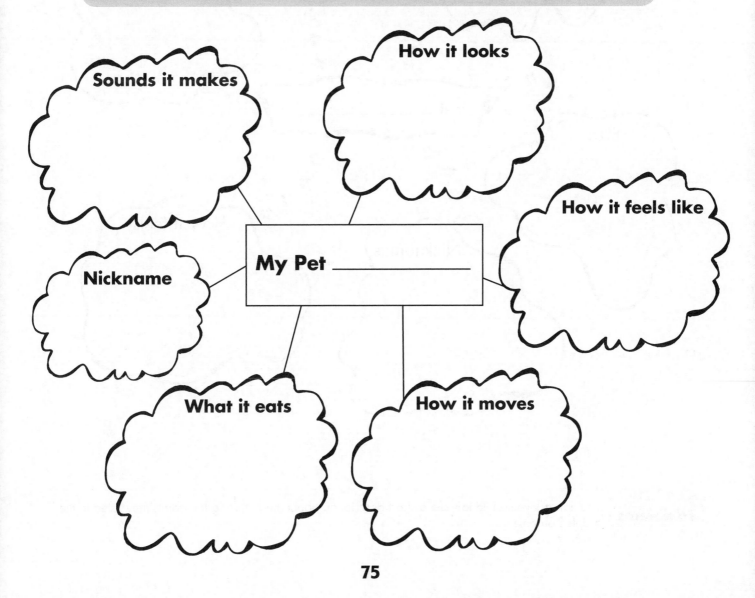

Sounds it makes

How it looks

How it feels like

Nickname

My Pet _____

What it eats

How it moves

B. Now, use the web below for ideas to write about a pet of your choice – real or make-believe. Include lots of details in each category.

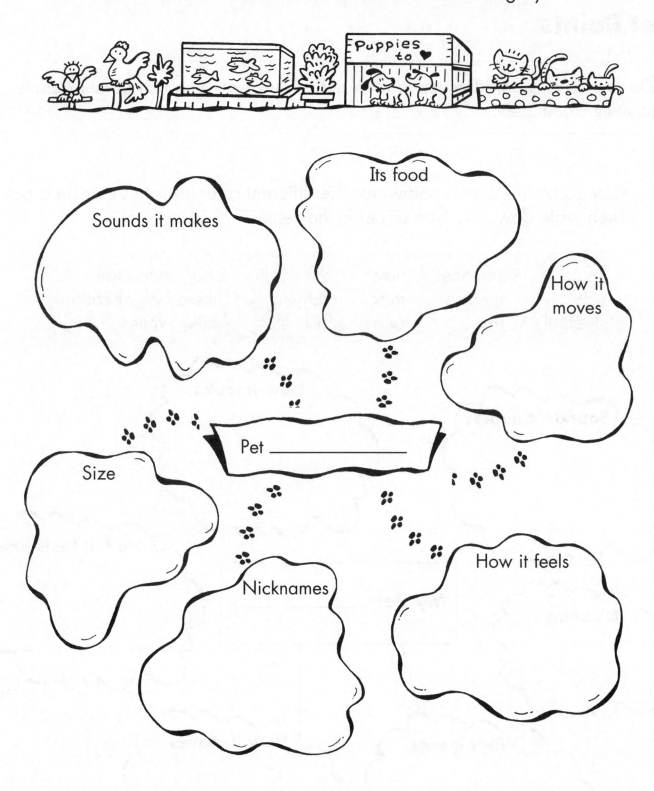

Its food

Sounds it makes

How it moves

Pet _____

Size

How it feels

Nicknames

To parents   You can ask your child to write a short description about the pet using the points they listed in the graphic organizer.

Detailed Descriptions

Good descriptive writing includes many details such as vivid sensory details. It often uses figurative language such as similes and metaphors, as well as precise verbs, adjectives and nouns to create a vivid image in the mind of the reader. When you organize a description, you can arrange it according to the sequence of events. When describing a person, think about the characteristics you want to focus on first.

A.	It is Teacher's Day and you want to write a tribute to your teacher. Think of a few characteristics of this teacher you are writing about and list them in the left column, using one box for each trait. In the corresponding right column, create and write down suitable elaborations to describe that trait.

Characteristic	Alliteration / Similes / Metaphors / Useful Phrases

B.	Use a graphic organizer of your own to organize your details in the space below:

C. Think about which characteristic you want to focus on first. When you are ready, write your tribute below. You may choose to address your teacher directly or to write a description of your teacher to be read out to the class.

_____

_____

_____

_____

_____

_____

_____

_____

_____

_____

_____

_____

_____

To parents You may want to get your child to type out the description and design it into a card with pictures or decorations.

Weather Words

People talk about the weather every day. You can use lots of weather words to describe a day.

Okay: The harbor was foggy.

Better: A damp fog slowly drifted into the harbor.

A.   List weather words for each weather condition. Think about weather reports you have seen or heard. Or look in the newspaper or at a weather website.

B. Look at the picture and list words or ideas that describe the scene.
    Use the question prompts to help you.

- What is happening to the trees?
- What is happening to the people?
- What is happening to the vehicles?

_____   _____

_____   _____

_____   _____

_____   _____

_____   _____

_____   _____

_____   _____

To parents Together with your child, write a short weather report that your child can present.

Add Character Traits

A **character** is someone who plays a part in a story or play. **Character traits** are the details that make a character unique. Planning a character ahead of time can help you when you write your stories.

A.   Can you think of some characters from books, television, songs or movies? Think about what you like or dislike about these characters. List the points or qualities below.

Character	Qualities I like
	Qualities I dislike

Character	Qualities I like
	Qualities I dislike

B. Make up a character for a story. Use this chart to plan your character.

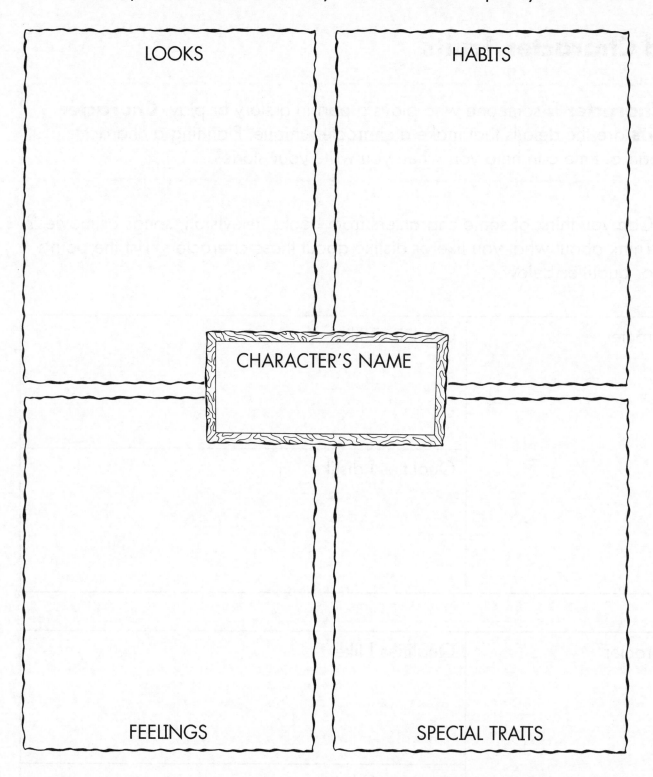

LOOKS

HABITS

CHARACTER'S NAME

FEELINGS

SPECIAL TRAITS

To parents Ask your child to draw a picture of the character to bring the character to life.

82

Dialogue Details

Dialogue is the words people say. You hear dialogue in movies and on TV. You read dialogue in stories and in plays. Comic book words are in dialogue 'bubbles'.

Read each sentence. It gives a main idea. Write words the characters say to get across that idea in the speech bubbles provided. Then, write the same dialogue on the lines provided in the next page. Remember to use quotation marks to separate the exact words of each speaker.

1. Two friends make plans to go on a picnic.

1: Expression – having a discussion

2: Expression – girl is suggesting something and boy is listening

3: Expression – one of them is asking a question

4: Expression – both of them smiling and talking

_____

_____

_____

_____

2.   A parent and child talk about moving to a new city.

1: Expression – mother telling the girl about moving to a new city

2: Expression – girl looks worried and raising her concerns

3: Expression – mother saying something reassuring to the girl

4: Expression – both of them talking and the girl looks more relaxed

To parents   Reproduce cartoon cells from comic strips without the dialogue and get your child to create the dialogue themselves.

Build a Sentence

A.   Pick a word or phrase from each column. Put them together to make a sentence.

Who / What?	Did what?	Where?	When?
a breeze	appeared	around town	after lunch
my cat	blared	at the clock	as night fell
his cousin	blew	from a tent	before dawn
the ghost	hid	near the zoo	during the show
that person	snored	on a fence	last week
a radio	wailed	under the porch	while we slept

1. _____

2. _____

3. _____

4. _____

5. _____

6. _____

B.   Pick one sentence you wrote. Rewrite it to make it better.

_____

_____

_____

C.   Now, build your own sentences. Write down ideas in the columns below. When you form your sentences, you may choose to take ideas from only some of the columns.

Who / What?	Did what?	Where?	When?	Why?

_____

_____

_____

_____

_____

D.   Pick one sentence you wrote. Read the following questions and rewrite your sentence to make it better.

- Can you use a more precise noun, vivid verb or adjective to help you?
- Can you use adverbs to make your sentence more lively?
- Can you add sensory details to your sentence?

_____

_____

_____

To parents   Create cards for each column so that your child can mix and match to build sentences.

Support a Main Idea

A **main idea** needs details that tell more about it. If a writer gave only main ideas, the writing would be dull and unclear.

Main Idea: It was a dark and stormy night.

Supporting Details: The moon hid behind thick clouds.
                       Harsh winds blew.

Read the sentences on pages 88 and 89. Each sentence gives a main idea. Sentences 1 to 3 are the topic sentences of the paragraphs. Write two more sentences that support the main idea. Use the pictures and questions to help you.

1.   The band was about to play its first show.

•   *What were the band members doing? How do you think they were feeling?*

_____

_____

_____

_____

_____

2. Local reporters waited to talk to the band.
   - *What were the reporters trying to do?*

   _____

   _____

   _____

   _____

   _____

3. The Monday paper had a great review of the show.
   - *What do think was reported in the papers? How do you think the band felt?*

   _____

   _____

   _____

   _____

   _____

Transition Train

Transition words link ideas. They give clues. Transition words show *how* and *why* ideas go together.

Okay: I wasn't hungry. I ate to be polite.

Better: I wasn't hungry, *but* I ate to be polite.

A. Read the idea in the train. Then read the transition word. Finish the sentence so that it makes sense.

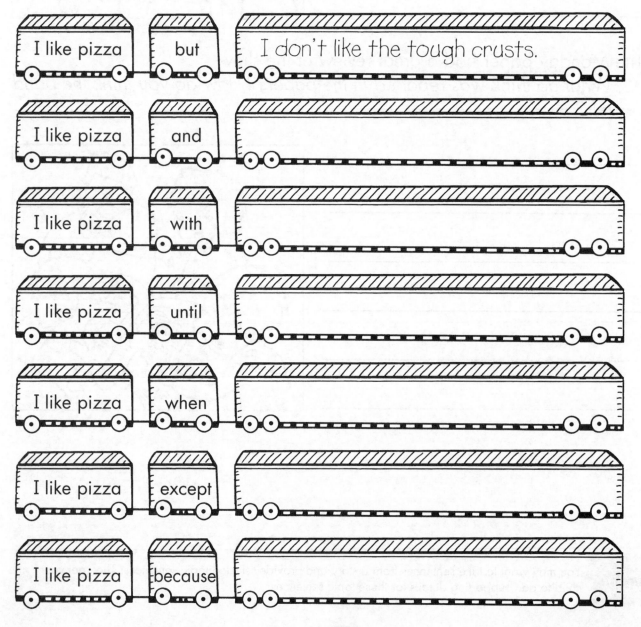

I like pizza | but | I don't like the tough crusts.

I like pizza | and

I like pizza | with

I like pizza | until

I like pizza | when

I like pizza | except

I like pizza | because

B. There are many types of transition words. A list of transition words and what they are used to signal is given below.

Transition words that show contrast	Transition words that show addition	Transition words that show order	Transition words that show time
Although	Also	First	When
However	Moreover	After	During
Rather	In addition	Later	Later
Still	Besides (this)	Next	Earlier
Even though	Furthermore	Finally	Little by little

Now, write one sentence each using a transition word from each list.

Transition word that shows contrast:

_____

Transition word that shows addition:

_____

Transition word that shows order:

_____

Transition word that shows time:

_____

Sentence Stretchers

Short sentences are fine – but not all the time. Sometimes sentences need more details. Use transition words as you add details.

Okay: Josh sang.

Better: Josh sang loudly while he rode his bike.

A.   Complete each sentence using the transition words and the pictures provided.

1.   Geraldine ran to her mother because

_____

_____

_____

2.   The bird was injured after _____

_____

_____

_____

3.   In addition, the bird was _____

_____

_____

_____

4.   Then, Geraldine quickly _____

_____

_____

B.   Read each sentence. Then stretch it by adding details. You may want to
     use the various transition words you have learned to add details.

1.   Rusty felt sick _____

_____

2.   Margo frowned _____

_____

3.   Kent needs a job _____

_____

4.   Devon chased the dog _____

_____

5.   Tonya has to leave early _____

_____

6.   The eagle swooped down _____

_____

Smooth Your Story

You can make a story better in many ways. One way is to smooth out choppy sentences.

Okay: I was sad. It was raining.
The TV didn't work. My dog wasn't around.

Better: I was sad that rainy Sunday.
The TV wasn't working and my trusty dog, Bruno, was at the vet.

A.   Read each story part. Use the helping questions to revise the sentences.

1.   The house was dark. It was eerie. We were scared.
   • What other details can you give about the house?
   • Instead of stating the feeling of being scared, can you describe a sensation?

_____

_____

2.   We heard noises. The noises were loud. Our ears hurt.
   • What kind of noises were these?
   • Can you use transition words to link the loud noises to the ears hurting?

_____

_____

3.   We saw a figure. The figure floated. We screamed.
   • How else can you describe this figure?
   • What else did the characters do when they saw the figure?

_____

_____

B. Read each part of the story. Make the parts flow together better. See the Smoothing Silo for hints.

1. The water was rough. The boat rocked. We groaned.

_____

_____

_____

2. It was hot. The window fogged up. It was hard to see.

_____

_____

_____

3. There was a loud noise. We drew back. We plugged our ears.

_____

_____

_____

4. It was 7 o'clock. Mom was jumpy. The phone rang.

_____

_____

_____

Precise Nouns

Vivid Verbs

Active Adjectives

Adverb Answers

Supporting Details

Spicy Synonyms

Character Traits

Sensory Details

Alliteration

Transitions

To parents   Ask your child to review some of their past writing and look for choppy sentences. Then get your child to suggest how they can smoothen their stories.

95

Exaggerate to Elaborate

When you exaggerate, you stretch the truth. Exaggeration makes things seem much bigger or smaller. It can make things seem much better or worse. Exaggeration can be funny or exciting.

Okay: Kenny was very hungry.

Better: Kenny wanted to eat 50 hot dogs and a watermelon.

A.   Read each description. How is each description an exaggeration? Write down the point you think the writer of each sentence was trying to make.

1.   The whole house shook with Dad's snoring.

_____

2.   I was melting under the heat.

_____

3.   We all walked around like blocks of ice.

_____

4.   She cried till she turned blue in the face.

_____

5.   I collected a whole ocean of water over those few rainy days.

_____

6. She could have fit an entire soccer team in her dress.

    _____

7. Not even an ant could get past that crack.

    _____

B. Make each sentence better by exaggerating. It's fine to be funny! The first one has been done for you.

1. The hat was too big on me. _The hat was so big, my whole family_

    could snuggle under it at the same time.

2. Hamid told a funny joke. _____

    _____

3. Sally had a sore throat. _____

    _____

4. We waited so long! _____

    _____

5. That was a dull game. _____

    _____

The Starting Line

A good starting sentence helps to capture your reader's attention. A dull beginning can bore your reader. You can begin your writing with:

- An impactful statement e.g. *It was one of those days you would not forget.*
- A question e.g. *Would you not have reacted the same way?*
- A command or request e.g. *"Do not come any further!"*
- An exclamation e.g. *Hurry into the house, the rain is coming!*

A. Create suitable starting sentences for the following topics using the above sentence types.

Topic: Shipwrecked!

Sentence Type: _____

Starting Sentence: _____

Topic: Away on a Trip

Sentence Type: _____

Starting Sentence: _____

Topic: That's Embarrassing!

Sentence Type: _____

Starting Sentence: _____

Topic: A Fabulous Party

Sentence Type: _____

Starting Sentence: _____

B. Select one of the topics in Part A and write a short story around it. Use the starting sentence you have written to begin your story and think up other types of starting sentences to begin your other paragraphs to make them more memorable.

_____

(Topic)

Beginning:

_____

_____

Middle:

_____

_____

_____

Ending:

_____

_____

Linking Paragraphs

Linking up your paragraphs is like tying them together so that your readers can see the connection between content in different paragraphs clearly. You can do so by using connecting words. Some examples of connecting words are:

also	although	finally	generally	however
instead	meanwhile	once	sometimes	soon

A. Read the paragraphs. Add connecting words to the beginning of the paragraphs to join them together. Use the words in the box above to help you.

Sean is an active boy. One of his favorite past-times is street surfing. He enjoys zipping around the neighborhood on his skateboard because he gets to meet many of his friends.

_____, Sean arranges to street surf with his friends. They will stop by one another's homes for snacks or for a break before continuing with their exploration.

_____, when it rains, Sean would prefer to stay indoors and paint while listening to his favorite pop songs. He enjoys watching the rain and painting whatever comes to his mind.

_____ of painting only at one particular area in the house, Sean would sometimes move around the living room to paint. He says he gets more inspiration that way.

_____ Sean enjoys both outdoor and indoor activities, what he loves most is to spend time with his family and his pet cat.

B. Read the first paragraph. Continue the writing by composing more paragraphs, using the helping words. Add connecting words to the beginning of these paragraphs to join them together into a complete piece of writing.

It was a typical day on a lazy weekend. Kayne was helping his father mow the lawn in the hot sun.

(cheerful boy, outdoors, breezy morning, cheerful attitude, chirpy whistling)

_____

_____

_____

(sister, new cake recipe, culinary skills, cooking expert)

_____

_____

_____

(delicious smells, tired but pleased, hard work, bath, lunch)

_____

_____

_____

To parents Get your child to continue the story by writing another paragraph. Ask him or her to use connecting words to join it to the other paragraphs.

Varying Sentences

Sentences in your writing should vary in length and variety just like spoken sentences in a conversation. Vary the length of your sentences by breaking up or combining sentences. You can add variety by reversing the order of ideas in a sentence, or changing statements into questions or exclamations.

A. Rewrite the following sentences to make them more interesting to read.

Example: I have school tomorrow.

1. By this time tomorrow, I will be back in school.
2. "Do I have to go back to school tomorrow?" I groaned.

1. The sky is blue.

_____

_____

2. I am not feeling well.

_____

_____

3. It is boring.

_____

_____

4. Our father is busy.

_____

_____

B. Paste a short article or paragraph from your newspapers or magazine in the space below. Read the sentences in it, then rewrite or reword them to make the article or paragraph better.

Paste your article or paragraph here:

C. Rewrite the paragraph here. Use the declarative, interrogative, imperative and exclamatory sentence types to vary your sentences. Vary their lengths to make them more conversational and easier to read.

_____

_____

_____

_____

_____

_____

_____

Eyewitness Elaborator

Reporters write about what they see, hear, and read. They take notes. Later, they turn the notes into a report. They elaborate to make the report clear.

A. Imagine that you are a reporter at a parade. Here are your notes. Expand the notes into good sentences.

July 4th parade passes Town Hall on way to River Park

_____
_____
_____

newest float for firefighters leads the way

_____
_____
_____

fire dogs march in red, white, and blue collars

_____
_____
_____

lively bands play favorite tunes

_____
_____
_____

best banner made by Bell Top School students

_____
_____
_____

B.   Now think of an event that you recently went to. It could be a school event or even an event you watched on TV. Write down some basic notes of what happened. Use the following questions to help you.

- When did the event take place?
- What was the event about?
- What happened during the event?
- How do you think the participants of the event felt?

_____   _____

_____   _____

_____   _____

C.   Use the notes that you have made of the event to write a short account of the event.

_____

_____

_____

_____

_____

_____

Writing a News Report

When writing a **news report**, use a graphic organizer to help you group information into related chunks. This will make your report neater and easier to understand.

A. Write a news report about the incident below. Gather your information using a graphic organizer and use it to help you write the report.

New Year's Day Congestion!

Scenario: On New Year's Day, many people were out celebrating. This caused quite a bit of traffic congestion on the roads and crowds at major attractions.

Write a short report about the above incident. Use the graphic organizer below to help you plan and write the report.

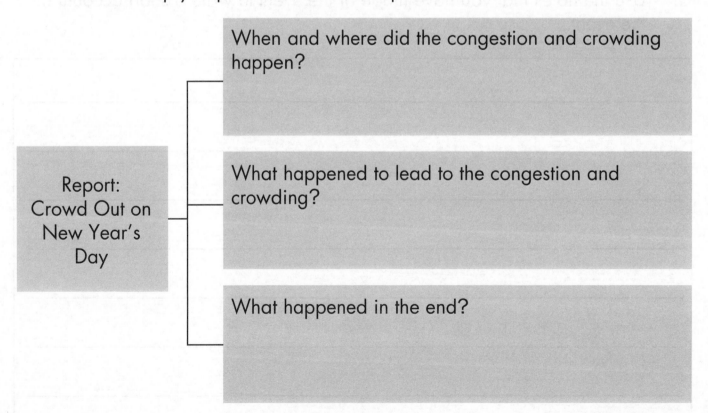

Report:
Crowd Out on
New Year's
Day

When and where did the congestion and crowding happen?

What happened to lead to the congestion and crowding?

What happened in the end?

B. Use the information you have written in the previous page to write your report. Remember to:
   - Use suitable connecting words to link up your paragraphs
   - Use a variety of sentence types
   - Vary your sentence lengths to make your report better

Crowd Out on New Year's Day!

_____

_____

_____

_____

_____

_____

_____

_____

_____

_____

_____

Date: _____

Add to an Ad

> An **ad** (short form for "advertisement") gives details about things people want to sell.
>
> *Okay:*   FOR SALE: Used bicycle, good condition
>
> *Better:*   FOR SALE: Girl's red bicycle; nearly new – used for only 2 months. Includes basket and bell.

A.   Read the following ads. Use the questions to improve each ad. You may add in other information if you choose to do so.

FOR SALE	FOR SALE
• Branded washing machine • 5kg load • Only 5 machines left!	

o   Is the machine front loading or top loading?
o   Where can customers get this machine?
o   What color is the machine? Is it brand new?

FOR SALE	FOR SALE
• Used books for sale! • This Saturday at 15 Burber Avenue	

o   What kind of books are on sale?
o   How many books are there? (You don't have to give an exact number.)
o   From what time to what time will the sale take place?

B. Imagine that you are having a yard sale. Write ads for four items to sell. Be honest. Give clear details. Get people interested.

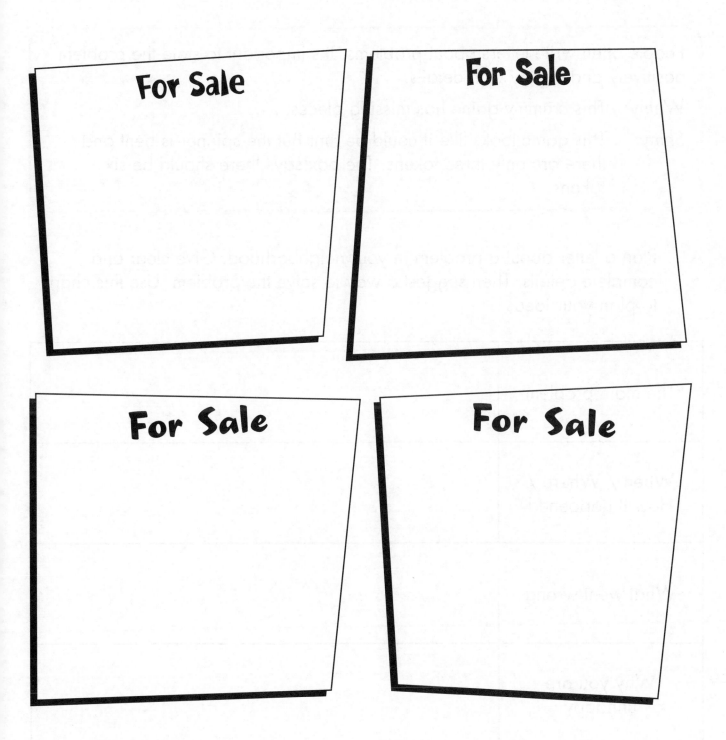

For Sale

For Sale

For Sale

For Sale

Don't Whine...Do Shine!

People often write letters about problems. It's important to state the problem positively and clearly with details.

Whiny: This crummy game has missing pieces.

Shiny: This game looks like it could be fun. But the spinner is bent and there are only three tokens. The box says there should be six tokens.

A.   Plan a letter about a problem in your neighborhood. Give clear and complete details. Then suggest a way to solve the problem. Use this chart to plan your ideas.

The main problem	
When / Where / How it happened	
What went wrong	
Why you are unhappy	
Possible solutions	

B. Now write a letter to your neighborhood organization to tell them about this problem. Remember to address them politely and thank them for their attention to this matter.

Dear _____,

_____

_____

_____

_____

_____

_____

_____

_____

_____

_____

Yours sincerely,

_____

Cooking Up a Recipe

When writing a **recipe**, it is important to record information accurately and in the right order. Use a graphic organizer to help you organize your information. List out the quantities of ingredients required. Number each step of the recipe and write it out using short and concise sentences.

A. Ask your family member or a friend to share with you a simple recipe. Make a voice recording or take down notes while he or she is telling you the recipe. Transfer the information from your notes or voice recording into the graphic organizer below.

This is a recipe for making _____.

The recipe makes _____ servings.

Ingredients and quantities required:

Ingredient preparation steps:

_____
Recipe

Cooking steps:

Serving suggestion:

112

B. Using the rearranged information from your graphic organizer, write out the recipe below.

_____

(Recipe title)

Makes ____ servings

You will need:

_____ _____

_____ _____

_____ _____

Cooking instructions:

1. _____

2. _____

3. _____

_____

_____

_____

_____

_____

To parents Try out the above recipe with your child. Make changes to parts of the recipe where procedures are not explained clearly to improve on it.

Cooking Up a Different Kind of Dish

A recipe does not always have to be about a dish. Sometimes you can write about a situation using the format of a recipe to provide instructions or directions for doing something.

A. Using the steps below, plan out instructions on one of the topics provided. Use your imagination to come up with creative ideas for your recipe. Choose one of the following topics:

1. A recipe for a loving family
2. A recipe for a lasting friendship

B. Plan your recipe in the graphic organizer below. Use the questions below to help you.

- What 'ingredients' do you think you would need, for example, would you need a whole lot of understanding and forgiveness to create a loving family?
- What 'steps' do you think are important? You could include steps like 'listening patiently' or 'talking kindly' as a step in creating a lasting friendship.

Ingredients and quantities required:

Steps:

_____
Recipe

Serving suggestion:

C. Using the rearranged information from your graphic organizer, write out the recipe below.

_____

(Recipe title)

You will need:

_____   _____

_____   _____

_____   _____

_____   _____

Steps:

1. _____

2. _____

3. _____

_____

_____

_____

_____

_____

To parents The above information can also be presented in the form of a paragraph instead of a recipe. Challenge your child to use the information and write it out in paragraph form.

Getting Somewhere!

The process of giving directions to a location is similar to that of writing a recipe. To get to your destination, you need to follow the directions in the correct order. Use a graphic organizer to help you organize information for your directions.

Decide on a place in your neighborhood that you wish to visit. Obtain a map or verbal instructions on how to get there from your house. Use a graphic organizer to sort out your information you have.

I want to go to _____.

You can paste the map or drawing of a map below. Then, number the steps on the image. Remember to provide landmarks for the reader to refer to. Each turning should be labeled as one step.

Now write your instructions below.

Starting Point: _____

Destination: _____

Travel mode: Walking / Cycling / Driving (Circle your mode of transport)

Directions:

1. _____

2. _____

3. _____

_____

_____

_____

_____

_____

_____

Elaboration Editor

The process of writing does not end with writing an essay. Often, we need to go through our work many times to check for errors and to improve our writing.

A. Read the following paragraph. Do you spot any errors? Circle the errors and write the corrections above.

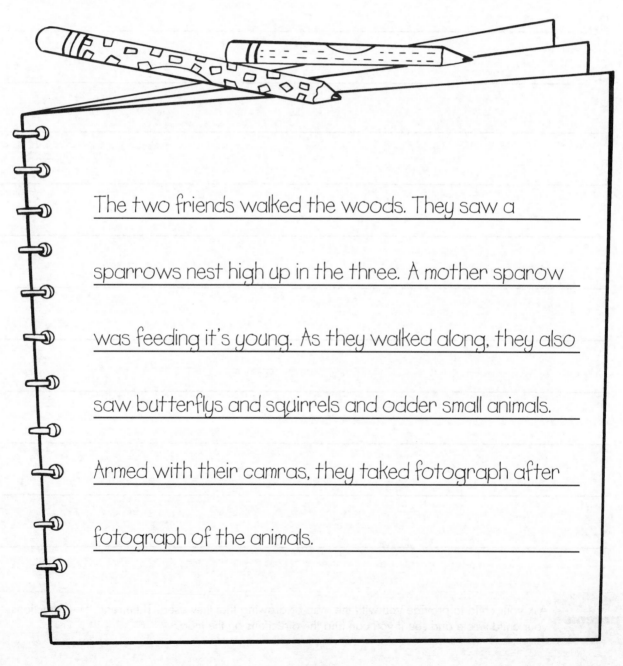

The two friends walked the woods. They saw a

sparrows nest high up in the three. A mother sparow

was feeding it's young. As they walked along, they also

saw butterflys and squirrels and odder small animals.

Armed with their camras, they taked fotograph after

fotograph of the animals.

B. Be an editor. Make this story better. Use the elaboration ideas you have learned. Write the new and improved story on a separate piece of paper.

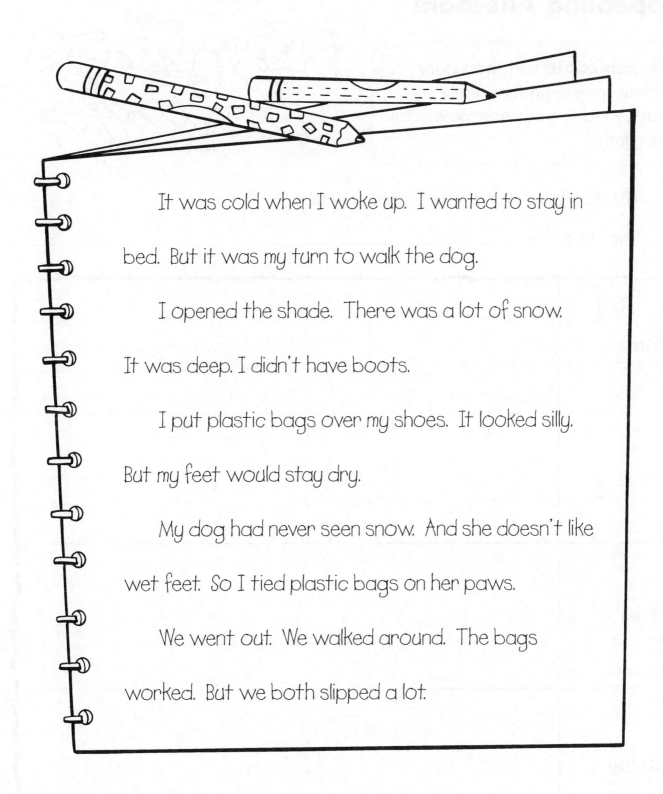

It was cold when I woke up. I wanted to stay in

bed. But it was *my* turn to walk the dog.

I opened the shade. There was a lot of snow.

It was deep. I didn't have boots.

I put plastic bags over *my* shoes. It looked silly.

But *my* feet would stay dry.

My dog had never seen snow. And she doesn't like

wet feet. So I tied plastic bags on her paws.

We went out. We walked around. The bags

worked. But we both slipped a lot.

Appealing Anecdote

> An **anecdote** is a short story about something that really happened to you. Anecdotes can be funny.

A. List details for an anecdote. Use the chart.

The Time That _____

First...	
Next...	
Then...	
At last...	

B.   Now use the details to write the anecdote.

_____

_____

_____

_____

_____

_____

_____

_____

_____

_____

_____

_____

_____

To parents Ask your child to think about how they might improve on their writing to make it more interesting and funny.

Elaborating

Let's round up the tips we have learnt in this book:

- Always support your main ideas with supporting ideas.

- Use your five senses to add details to your descriptions.

- Use elaboration techniques such as alliteration, similes and metaphors to give refreshing descriptions of people and things.

- Use vivid verbs, nouns, adjectives and adverbs to make your descriptions clearer.

- Vary the length of your sentences.

- Use connecting words or sentences to link your paragraphs.

A.   Let's put together all the things you have learnt into one great piece of writing. Let's start by deciding what kind of story you want to create.

Circle your choice of story and narrative voice:

   I want to create a happy / scary / humorous / touching story.

   I will write it in the first / third person narrative.

Now, draw and use a suitable graphic organizer to plan your writing.

B. Let's write your story here. Remember to use connecting words and sentences to join up your paragraphs:

_____

(Title)

Introduction / First Paragraph:

_____

_____

_____

Middle:

_____

_____

_____

_____

_____

_____

_____

Ending / Last Paragraph:

_____

_____

_____

To parents Teach your child how to write a good story by going through the above steps with him or her. While you are doing it, remember to guide your child using what has been taught in this book.

123

Test Prep Tips

When you write a passage for a test, remember to do the following:

* Read all directions carefully and completely.

* Give yourself a few moments to think and plan.

* Make notes or use graphic organizers to get started. Group ideas that go together.

* Before you write, cross out ideas you don't need.

* Stick to your topic.

* Support main ideas with details.

* Use elaboration ideas as you go. Prompt yourself.

* Read over what you have written before you turn it in.

* Even if you cannot read aloud during the test, read slowly and silently to yourself.

* Fix any errors you notice. Check spelling, capitalization, and punctuation.

* Be sure your handwriting is clear.

Self-Prompting Hints

Read your writing out loud. Listen to yourself.

- ❏ Does it sound right?

- ❏ Did I leave out a word?

- ❏ Did I use the same words too many times?

- ❏ Do I need more details?

- ❏ Could I write an idea more clearly?

- ❏ Do my sentences flow smoothly?

- ❏ Does my writing sound interesting?

Listen to your own voice.

- ❏ If I *stop*, did I use a <u>period</u>?

- ❏ If I *pause*, did I use a <u>comma</u>?

- ❏ If my voice *rises*, did I use a <u>question mark</u>?

Read your whole story.

- ❏ Will it grab a reader's attention?

- ❏ Does the story paint a clear picture?

- ❏ Will readers be able to tell the characters apart?

- ❏ Does the dialogue sound like how people really speak?

- ❏ Does it have a clear ending?

Elaboration Self-Evaluation Checklist

Look over what you have written.
Ask yourself: *Have I...*

- ❑ used precise nouns?

- ❑ used vivid verbs?

- ❑ added active adjectives?

- ❑ added adverbs to answer questions?

- ❑ replaced tired words like *thing* and *nice*?

- ❑ written clear and complete sentences?

- ❑ written smooth sentences?

- ❑ written lively dialogue?

- ❑ used better synonyms?

- ❑ used alliteration?

- ❑ used similes?

- ❑ added sensory details?

- ❑ given details to support a main idea?

- ❑ described characters?

- ❑ used transition words?

Reread your work one more time.
Ask yourself: *Have I...*

- ❑ grabbed the reader's attention?

- ❑ done my best to make my writing strong and clear?

Answers

Pages 6–7
A. animal – lion, dolphin, pig, camel, hippopotamus
   clothing – evening grown, jacket, trousers, tie, blouse, raincoat
   drink – milkshake, coffee, fruit juice, lemonade, tea
   house – terrace, mansion, bungalow
   person – pirate, student, singer, journalist, engineer, teacher, princess, doctor
B. 1. I ate spicy peppers.
   2. The eagle flew so high.
   3. That old kite lost its tail.
   4. You need a hammer to fix it.
   5. She liked the book's red jacket.
   6. Let's make a play castle.
   7. Jen used to play the flute in the orchestra.

Pages 8–13 *Accept reasonable answers.*

Pages 14–15
These are suggested answers.
A. boy – poor, malnourished, sad
   weather – chilly, windy, wintery
B. tree – shady, leafy, stout, green
   cloud – white, scenic, silky

Pages 16–17 *Accept reasonable answers.*

Pages 18–19
A. 1. excited, wild, overjoyed
   2. high, towering, gigantic
   3. loud, harsh, deafening
B. *These are suggested answers.*
   • famished, parched, terrified
   • peckish, dry, startled
   • arid, hungry, scared

Pages 20
These are suggested answers.
1. The desert receives very little rain.
2. Desert animals usually burrow themselves deep in the sand.
3. The roots of desert plants are usually very long and lie close to the surface so that they can quickly catch water from the rain.
4. Lizards always sleep at night.
   Or Lizards never sleep during the day.
5. The desert always feels hot.

6. You can't see clearly in the desert because of dust and haze.

Pages 21–23
A. 1. diligently 2. boastfully 3. dreamily 4. triumphantly
   5. bravely 6. doubtfully 7. hungrily 8. longingly
B. *These are suggested answers.*
   2. comfortably 3. expertly 4. slyly 5. painstakingly
   6. energetically 7. correctly 8. devotedly 9. eagerly
   10. jovially
C. *These are suggested answers.*
   • beautifully, busily, carefully, closely, delightedly
   • impatiently, moodily, cheerfully, resignedly, helpfully

Pages 24–25
A. angrily, calmly, cautiously, eagerly, exasperatedly, gladly, happily, hastily, loudly, politely, quietly, rudely, softly, suddenly, thoughtfully, warmly
B. *Accept reasonable answers.*

Pages 26–29 *Accept reasonable answers.*

Pages 30–31
A. Synonyms for HAPPY – thrilled, jolly, contented, joyful, pleased, cheery, glad, blissful
   Synonyms for PERSON – anyone, human, being, creature, somebody, member, character
   Synonyms for COLD – chilly, wintry, frosty, frozen, arctic, nippy
B. Synonyms for RUN – jog, dash, sprint, scurry
   Synonyms for WALK – stroll, tread, saunter, wander, stride
   Synonyms for SCREAM – howl, yell, shriek, screech, shout
   Synonyms for LAUGH – giggle, chuckle, cackle, guffaw
   Synonyms for EAT – swallow, gobble, munch
   Synonyms for JUMP – bounce, skip, leap, hop

Page 32 *Accept reasonable answers.*

Pages 33–34
A. Across: 2. Nice 4. Error 6. Mad 7. Mighty
   9. Beautiful
   Down: 1. Lie 3. Comical 5. Rot 8. Glad 10. True
B. Across: 1. Won 2. Sat 3. Slept 4. Sad 5. Cried
   Down: 1. Walked 2. Steal

Pages 35–37

A. Antonyms for PLEASANT – unkind, nasty, spiteful, unfriendly, hostile

Antonyms for SUCCESS – failure, disappointment, flop, catastrophe, let down

Antonyms for COLD – loving, warm, kind, tender, sincere, friendly

B and C. *Accept reasonable answers.*

Pages 38–39

A. Across: 2. Timid 4. Proud 7. Succeed 8. Easy
Down: 1. Big 3. Shallow 8. Loud 6. Rude

B. *Accept reasonable answers.*

Pages 40–41

A. 1. buddies 2. sisters 3. siblings 4. crowded 5. space
6. hideaway 7. lumber 8. furniture 9. build
10. entrance 11. furniture 12. eagerly 13. homey
14. cushions 15. hosted

B. *Accept reasonable answers.*

Pages 42–43 *Accept reasonable answers.*

Pages 44–45

A. *These are suggested answers.*
2. Neat Ned 3. Talkative Terry 4. Grumpy Grandpa
5. Proud Priscilla 6. Fast Fred

B. *Accept reasonable answers.*

Pages 46–47 *Accept reasonable answers.*

Pages 48–49

A. 2. Eats like a bird 3. Fighting like cats and dogs
4. Busy bee 5. Ivory skin 6. Wise as an owl

B and C. *Accept reasonable answers.*

Pages 50–51

A. 1. He was frozen with fear in the haunted house.
2. It has been raining cats and dogs since yesterday.
3. Those mean words that Joe said were daggers through my heart.
4. Bob is the shining star of our school.
5. The wonderful news sent my heart racing.

B. *Accept reasonable answers.*

Pages 52–64

Accept reasonable answers.

Pages 65–66

A. 1. for Childern's Day. 2. all around the compound.
3. because they all wanted to get the prizes. 4. to look for the prizes the teachers hid. 5. as everyone got a prize.

B and C. *Accept reasonable answers.*

Pages 67–74 *Accept reasonable answers.*

Pages 75–76

A. My pet: Cat
How it looks: tiny, fluffy, short round tail, milky white
How is feels like: soft, like a ball of cotton
How is moves: stealthily, pounces
Nickname: Snowball   What it eats: milk, fish, biscuits
Sound it makes: meows, yelps, purrs

B. *Accept reasonable answers.*

Pages 77–89 *Accept reasonable answers.*

Pages 90–91

A. I like pizza and pasta. / I like pizza with lots of cheese. / I like pizza until there is some other option to eat. / I like pizza when my mother has cooked vegetables. / I like pizza except having it for breakfast. / I like pizza because it is easily available.

B. *Accept reasonable answers.*

Pages 92–93

A. 1. Geraldine ran to her mother because she found an injured bird.
2. The bird was injured after it fell off its nest.
3. In addition, the bird was attacked by a cat.
4. Then, Geraldine quickly picked up the bird and shooed the cat away.

B. 1. Rusty fell sick again because he was not taking precaution.
2. Margo frowned as she read the letter.
3. Kent needs a job in order to feed his family.
4. Devon chased the dog away as it was trying to steal meat from his shop.
5. Tonya has to leave early in order to make it to the airport on time.
6. The eagle swooped down to pick its prey.

Pages 94–99 *Accept reasonable answers.*

Pages 100–101

A. Sometimes / However / Instead / Although

B. *Accept reasonable answers.*

Pages 102–117 *Accept reasonable answers.*

Pages 118–119

A. The two friends walked **into** the woods. They saw a **sparrow's** nest high up in the **tree**. A mother sparow was feeding **its** young. As they walked along, they also saw **butterflies,** squirrels and **other** small animals. Armed with their **cameras,** they **took photograph** after **photograph** of the animals.

B. *Accept reasonable answers.*

Pages 120–123 *Accept reasonable answers.*